OUR PLACES OF WORSHIP

Hinduism

Honor Head

WAYLAND

First published in 2009
by Wayland

Copyright © Wayland 2009

Wayland
338 Euston Road
London NW1 3BH

Wayland Australia
Level 17/207 Kent Street
Sydney NSW 2000

Commissioning editor: Jennifer Sanderson
Editor: Jean Coppendale
Designer: Paul Manning
Consultant: Beryl Dhanjal, lecturer and writer
    on South Asian history and religions

British Library Cataloguing in Publication Data
Head, Honor.
    Hinduism. — (Our places of worship)
    1. Temples, Hindu—Juvenile literature.
    2. Public worship—
    Hinduism—Juvenile literature.
    3. Hinduism—Juvenile literature.
    I. Title II. Series
    294.5'35-dc22

ISBN: 978 0 7502 4929 4

This book can be used in conjunction with the interactive CD-Rom, *Our Places of Worship*. To do this, look for ⊙ and the file path. For example, material on mandirs can be found on ⊙ Hinduism/Mandirs/Types of Mandirs. From the main menu of the whiteboard, click on 'Hinduism', then 'Mandirs' and then 'Types of Mandirs'.

To see a sample from the CD-Rom, log on to www.waylandbooks.co.uk.

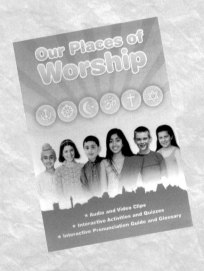

Our Places of Worship
Single user licence: ISBN 978 0 7502 5303 1
School library service licence: ISBN 978 0 7502 5532 5
Site user licence: ISBN 978 0 7502 5533 2

Picture credits
l = left r = right t = top b= bottom
Cover, 5, 6, 7, 8, 9, 13, 14, 15, 17, 20t, 21 Discovery Media/Our Places of Worship;
4 jorisvo/Shutterstock; 10 Dinodia Photo Library/ArkReligion.com; 11 Kharidehal Abhirama
Ashwin/Shutterstock; 12 David Clegg/ArkReligion.com; 16 Helene Rogers/ArkReligion.com;
18 Mark Pearson/Alamy; 19 Robert Harding Picture Library Ltd/Alamy; 20b Mahesh Patil/
Shutterstock; 22 Lindsay Hebberd/Corbis; 23t Dallas Events Inc/Shutterstock; 23b Andreanna
Seymore/Getty; 24 Tim Gainey/Alamy; 25, 26 Louise Batalla Duran/Alamy; 27 epa/Corbis;
28, 29 Regien Paassen/Shutterstock

Printed in China

Wayland is a division of Hachette Children's Books,
an Hachette UK company.
www.hachette.co.uk

Contents

Words appearing in **bold**, like this, can be found in the glossary on pages 30.

What is a mandir?

A mandir, or temple, is where Hindus go to worship. Hindus follow a religion called **Hinduism** that began in India. It is one of the world's oldest religions. Some of the old mandirs in India are richly decorated and have colourful carvings on the outside.

▼ Each figure on the outside of this mandir tells a story to Hindus.

Mandirs around the world

Many Hindu communities build their own mandir. In some countries, Hindus have changed old buildings that were used for schools or homes into mandirs. This means they may look very different from the mandirs in India and other parts of Asia.

Brahman

Hindus believe that there is only one God, called **Brahman**, although he can appear in many different forms. Each form is called a **deity** and each deity has special powers, such as bringing wealth, luck, peace or happiness. Many mandirs are dedicated to one deity.

▲ The Gujarat Hindu Society community centre in Preston, England, has a mandir where Hindus go to worship.

WHAT DO YOU THINK?

Why do you think some communities like to build their own mandir?

◀ The Shri Geeta Bhawan mandir in Birmingham, England, used to be a church. It became a mandir in 1967.

Welcome to the mandir

Hindus call worship puja. Hindus can worship at the mandir at any time of the day, but many people like to go in the early morning or the evening. Mandirs have a bell outside or just inside the doorway that worshippers ring before they enter. Hindus always take off their shoes when they enter the mandir. This is done as a sign of respect for God and to keep the mandir clean. Puja is led by the temple priest, or pujari.

▶ Each mandir is looked after by a priest, who often lives in one of the rooms there.

The shrine room

In the shrine room there is a raised platform called a shrine with a statue or picture of the deity on it. Worshippers bow down in front of the deity and give offerings of flowers, fruit or **incense** as a sign of their respect for the deities. The shrine has a curtain around it. The priest opens the curtain so that the people can see the deity. Seeing the deity is called 'darshan' in **Hindi**.

◀ Worshippers bow down in front of the deities on the shrine. The deities here are Sita (left), Rama (middle) and Lakshman (right).

⊙ Hinduism/Mandirs/Inside the Mandirs

Special lamp

Men and women sit together during puja. Everyone who can, sits on the floor. The priest performs the arti ceremony to show everyone's love for God. He lights a special lamp and waves it in front of the deities to make the flame from the lamp **sacred**. Then he takes the lamp to the worshippers, who move their hands over the flame to receive **blessings** from the deities.

▲ The priest holds the lamp that is used for the arti ceremony.

Prayers and songs

During puja, the priest reads from an important Hindu holy book called the **Bhagavad Gita** (see page 19). Then worshippers sing songs to praise God. These songs are called bhajans. The worshippers also say prayers including one called the Gayatri Mantra, which asks God to guide them to act and think in the right way.

▼ Part of puja is to say prayers asking God for guidance.

Eating together

During puja, the priest offers some food to the deity. This food is called prashad. It can be a mix of nuts, dried fruit and sugar or a big, cooked meal. The food is then shared between the worshippers.

▲ Everyone eats some prashad that, they believe, has been blessed by the deity.

THE PRIEST

The priest at the mandir performs a variety of different duties. As well as leading the worship, he will give advice to members of the local community. He might also talk to people who want to learn more about Hinduism.

▶ Talking to people about the teachings of Brahman is an important job for the priest.

What Hindus believe

Hindus believe that a person's **soul** lasts forever, unlike their body, which will die and rot away. They believe that when they die, their soul enters another body. This body could be a person, an animal or a plant. This is called reincarnation, which means being born again. The form the new body takes depends on how good the person was in this life.

▶ This painting shows the same person being reborn many times, including as a woman, a warrior and a **scholar**.

One with God

Hindus believe that when their soul is good enough, it will become one with God and they will not be reincarnated anymore. They seek to achieve this 'oneness' through loving God, worship, **meditation**, and living and behaving well.

Respect for all

Hindu teaching is that all living things have a soul and so they must be respected and treated kindly. When Hindus meet, they put the palms of their hands together and say 'namaste', which means 'my respects to you'.

▼ Hindus greet each other with the word 'namaste' to show their respect.

WHAT DO YOU THINK?

Why do you think respect is an important part of behaving well?

What can happen when there is no respect between people?

Brahman and the deities

Hindus believe that Brahman is all around, everywhere, all the time. There are many different forms of Brahman. These forms are called deities. Hindus choose one or some of the deities to love and respect, but each deity is a part of Brahman.

▶ Brahma is a form of Brahman. Hindus believe Brahma made the world.

⊙ Hinduism/Worship

Dressing the deity

Each mandir has statues and pictures of their deity. The statue of the deity is usually washed and dressed each morning. During the day, offerings are made to the deity. At night, it is put to bed. This is a sign of love for the deity and Brahman. Incense is kept on the shrine so that the air around the deity is always clean and sweet.

◀ Each day, the priest dresses the statue of Lord Rama and leaves fresh flowers on the shrine.

tray for incense

offerings

The deities

Three of the most well-known deities are Brahma, the creator, Vishnu who protects and looks after the world, and Lord Shiva who destroys all evil. Shakti, Shiva's wife, is also a powerful deity. She is usually gentle and kind but can be fierce when she is protecting something that is precious to her.

WHAT DO YOU THINK?

Why do you think it is good to have lots of different forms of one God?

If you could choose one deity to worship, which one would it be?

Krishna

Many of the deities can appear in different forms. One of the most well-loved is Lord Krishna, who is a form of Vishnu. Lord Krishna is brave, loyal and clever. He is often shown playing a flute and wearing a crown decorated with a peacock feather and jewels.

▲ Krishna is usually shown with Radha. The love they have for each other is a symbol of the love that people should have for God.

Ganesh

Each deity has a different power or responsibility. Hindus believe that Ganesh, the elephant-headed deity, brings good luck. Lakshmi is the deity of good fortune, beauty and success. Many Hindu shops and offices have a statue of Ganesh or Lakshmi.

▶ Ganesh helps people to achieve their goals and brings them good luck.

Rama and Sita

Lord Rama is the hero of the great Hindu story, the Ramayana (see page 19). Rama is a good and brave warrior and always does the right thing. He is married to Sita, his loyal wife.

◀ Rama is another form of Vishnu. He teaches Hindus how to be brave and honest. His marriage to Sita shows perfect love.

Worshipping at home

Many Hindu families worship every day at home. They usually have a special place in their house where they keep a shrine with pictures or statues of their favourite deity. They usually perform puja in the early morning, as Hindus believe they then start each new day with God's blessing. Worshippers always wash their hands and feet before puja.

◀ Special puja trays with candles and arti lamps are sold for worshippers to use at home.

Ringing the bell

Just as they do in the mandir, Hindus worshipping at home begin by ringing a bell and then bowing in front of the shrine. They burn incense on the shrine and leave offerings of fruit and flowers. Some people may light an arti lamp so they can perform the blessings ceremony.

WHAT DO YOU THINK?

What are the differences between a mandir and worshipping at home?

Do you think one is better than the other? Why?

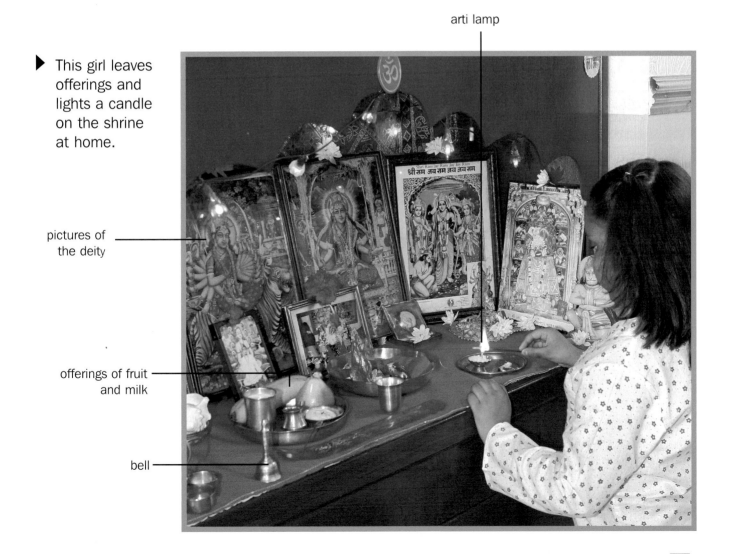

▶ This girl leaves offerings and lights a candle on the shrine at home.

arti lamp

pictures of the deity

offerings of fruit and milk

bell

Holy books

Hindus have many holy books. Some of these contain stories about the deities and others teach Hindus about right and wrong. Most of the books are written in an ancient language called **Sanskrit**. Not many Hindus can read this language so the books are often read aloud by priests, or parts of them are performed as films or plays.

The Ramayana

The Ramayana is a story about the deity Lord Rama and his wife, Sita. Rama's evil stepmother sent them to live in a forest where Sita was kidnapped by a demon. She was rescued and Rama and Sita were eventually made king and queen. The story is about bravery, loyalty and everlasting love.

▶ Many stories from the Hindu holy books are performed as plays. This scene is from the Ramayana.

▲ This scene from the Ramayana shows the battle between good and evil.

The Bhagavad Gita

The Hindu book, Bhagavad Gita, means 'song of God'. This is one of the most popular books and also the holiest scripture in Hinduism. Hindus believe that it is a message from Vishnu, telling them that God should be at the centre of their lives. It also explains how they should behave each day.

The Mahabharata

The Mahabharata is the story of Lord Krishna. It tells of major battles between princes and deities for power. It is a way of explaining how Hindus should behave towards God and each other. The story has been made into films and plays.

WHAT DO YOU THINK?

Why is it a good idea to explain religious teachings through a story or film?

Signs and symbols

The main religious symbols in Hinduism are the Aum and the swastika. The Aum, or Om, sign stands for Brahman, or God. It is often used to decorate the outside of mandirs so that people know the building is a place for Hindu worship. It is also a sacred sound which Hindus say at the beginning and end of their prayers.

▲ The Aum symbol is used to decorate mandirs and shrines. Hindus also chant the word to help them meditate.

Symbol of good luck

The swastika is a symbol of good fortune. In Hindi, the word swastika means 'all is well'. The symbol is used in Hindu art and **architecture** and as a decoration. Banners with the swastika are displayed during Hindu festivals and at special ceremonies, such as weddings.

swastika —

▶ The swastika symbol has been put on this rug as a decoration and a sign of good luck.

☉ Hinduism/Signs, Symbols and Religious Objects

Red mark

When Hindus worship they wear a red mark on their forehead called a tilak. The tilak is a sign of a blessing from God. It is made from red paste or powder. The tilak mark is made on each person's forehead before they start puja.

WHAT DO YOU THINK?

Why do you think signs and symbols are important?

How do you think a religious symbol should be used?

tilak

▶ The priest wears the tilak when he is in the mandir during puja.

Special occasions

Worship and receiving God's blessings are an important part of a Hindu's life. At the age of one year, a Hindu baby has his or her first haircut. The parents take the baby to the local mandir where the priest performs a special puja and shaves the baby's head. This ceremony is called Chudakarana.

▼ At the Chudakarana ceremony, the priest rings a bell. He then shaves away any hair with which the baby was born. The child can now grow new hair to symbolise a fresh start.

Wedding ceremony

A traditional Hindu wedding can last for weeks and includes lots of different ceremonies and services. An important part of the service takes place around a sacred fire. In some parts of the world, such as India, this happens outside. In many countries, such as Britain and the United States, a small fire may be lit in a container inside the mandir. The bride and groom take seven steps and make seven promises to each other for a long and happy marriage.

MEHNDI ART

Using **henna** to decorate the bride's hands and feet is a traditional part of a Hindu wedding. The bride meets with her friends the day before the wedding ceremony to have her hands and feet decorated with beautiful patterns.

▲ This Indian form of body art is called mehndi.

◀ Most Hindu brides wear red on their wedding day as a sign that they will have a big and happy family. This bride is praying with the priest as part of the ceremony.

Hindu festivals

Divali is known as the festival of lights and is a very important Hindu festival. It celebrates the homecoming of Rama and Sita from their time in the forest (see page 18). The festival celebrates the victory of light or good over darkness and evil. Just before Divali, Hindus clean and decorate their homes and mandirs. They light a lot of candles and lamps before performing a special puja at home or in the mandir.

▶ For Divali, many Hindus paint special patterns, called **rangoli**, on the ground outside their homes. These are to attract the deities and keep evil spirits away.

Festival of colours

The festival of Holi celebrates the beginning of spring. Hindus build large bonfires to remember the burning of the witch, Holika, and the triumph of good over evil. Hindus also spray each other with coloured powder and water. This is to remember Krishna playing tricks on his friends by throwing water over them.

HOLIKA AND PRINCE PRAHLAD

Prince Prahlad's father was King and wanted everyone to worship him. When Prahlad said he would only worship Vishnu, the King ordered Holika to kill him. Holika had special powers and could not die. She tricked Prahlad into sitting on her lap in an unlit bonfire and then set the bonfire alight. Because she was using her special powers for evil, she was burnt to death but Prahlad walked away unharmed.

▼ During Holi, children throw coloured water and powder over each other to celebrate.

Durga Puja

Many Hindu festivals celebrate important events in the lives of the deities. Durga is a deity who killed a wicked demon to save her people. Her festival, Durga Puja, lasts for nine days. During this time, Hindus worship at home and in the mandirs. In many parts of India there are carnivals and street processions.

▼ In the mandir, a priest makes puja before a statue of Durga, during the festival of Durga Puja.

▼ In many parts of India there are huge parades to celebrate Ganesh's birthday.

Lord Krishna's birthday

In August or September, the festival of Janmashtami celebrates the birthday of Lord Krishna. At this time Hindus **fast** and, in the mandir, the priest reads stories about Krishna and his life. Statues of Krishna as a baby are put on display in the mandirs and food offerings are made to the baby Krishna.

Ganesh's birthday

Ganesh brings success with new beginnings. Hindus ask for his blessing if they move into a new home or start a new job. On his birthday, Hindus in many parts of India carry a huge statue of Ganesh down to the sea or river and let it go in the water.

Holy places

Most Hindu holy sites are places that were visited by one of the deities. The holiest place for many Hindus is the city of Varanasi in northern India. There are hundreds of mandirs here. The main mandir is devoted to Lord Shiva. Millions of **pilgrims** travel to Varanasi each year.

▼ Hindus believe that if a person dies in Varanasi, he or she will go straight to Heaven and will not be reincarnated.

Holy river

For Hindus, the River Ganges in India is holy. Thousands of people bathe in it every day and believe that it can wash away all their sins. Hindus believe the river comes from the deity, Ganga, and that the water carries blessings from all the other deities. Some Hindus keep water from the Ganges at home to give to someone who is ill. When Hindus die, their bodies are often floated down the River Ganges or their ashes are scattered onto the water.

WHAT DO YOU THINK?

Why do you think certain places are holy to some people?

Why do you think people travel a long way to visit these holy places?

▼ Indians use the River Ganges for washing, and also travel on it by rowing boat. Hindus believe the water is holy and blessed by the deities.

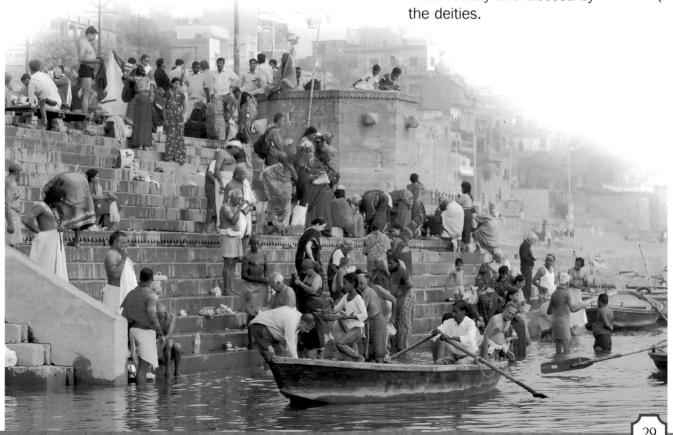

Glossary

architecture the style or way a building is made

Bhagavad Gita the holiest scripture in Hinduism. This story teaches Hindus how to behave

blessings holy thoughts that bring happiness and are believed to be passed from the deities to worshippers

Brahman the one and only Hindu God who is everywhere, all the time

deity a form of Brahman, or God, such as Ganesh, the elephant-headed deity

fast when someone does not eat or drink for a certain time

ghee a type of oil made from butter, used a lot in Indian cooking

henna a dye that is used to colour and decorate the skin

Hindi the language spoken by Hindus

Hinduism the name of the religion followed by Hindus

incense sticks of sweet-smelling perfume and spices that are burnt on Hindu shrines

pilgrims people who go on special journeys to holy places

meditation to sit quietly and calmly, and clear the mind of everyday thoughts

rangoli a type of art, usually made of patterns and shapes drawn with white and coloured powders

sacred something that is holy

Sanskrit an ancient Indian language. Many holy books are written in Sanskrit

scholar someone who spends a lot of time studying and reading books

soul part of a person that cannot be seen or touched but that makes the person feel and think the way they do

Quizzes

Try these quizzes to see how much you remember about Hinduism.

Are these facts true or false?

1. A mandir is a place where Hindus worship.

2. Hindus believe Krishna is the one true God.

3. The deity Ganesh has an elephant's head.

4. Before they enter the mandir, worshippers knock on the door.

5. Part of the priest's job is to dress the deity each day.

Can you match the names below to the special objects on the shrine?

a. arti lamp

b. bell

c. picture of the deity

d. offerings to the deity

Answers are on the next page.

Index

Answers

1 True
2 False, Krishna is a deity but Brahman is the one true God
3 True
4 False, they ring a bell
5 True

Match the names to the objects: a3, b4, c2, d1

OUR PLACES OF WORSHIP

Contents of titles in the series:

WAYLAND